UNTIL THE LAST PETAL FALLS

BY

DENISE TAYLOR

Dedicated

to

our angel babies

Contents

Until the last petal falls

Prologue

Once upon a time

Once upon a time, in a faraway land, was the idea of the perfect conception…unfortunately not the case for my fairy tale.

A Fairy tale is a short story typically featuring Fairy's, Mermaid's, Unicorns, Magic & Enchantment. Mine features needles, medications, scans and numerous trips to the hospital, although there are unicorns (I will explain later) and I am holding on for the magic and the happy ever after.

So, who am I??

Why write a book??

Why tell the world my journey??

I am just a regular girl who is on an incredibly hard journey and trying to find ways to get me through day to day and hoping that by sharing my thoughts, feelings and experiences along the way I can help others too. If this only reaches one person, it will be worth it. It has helped me vent out the craziness that goes on in your mind when you go through

IVF, people on this journey will understand the craziness!

I am incredibly nervous but very excited to share my journey with you and hope you stay with me until the fairy tale ends.... hopefully with our happy ever after.

Chapter 1

Belle

"**Belle**" I know what you're thinking, strange title right? What's it got to do with IVF? What's it got to do with my journey?? Well let me explain...

...Belle means beauty, beautiful woman, dream, vision and many more synonyms I won't bore you by listing. Beautiful woman goes beyond a woman's looks, it's their physical and mental strength, their soul, their ability to rebuild themselves and comeback stronger whilst armed with their weaknesses, their ability to carry on regardless.

When I first started my IVF journey, I knew it wasn't going to be an easy ride, I knew I would need to be strong, but I never quite realized how strong. It affects you in so many ways you just wouldn't believe, the physical strain, the mental strain, the emotions (oh god the emotions!!!) the strain on your loved ones, protecting them from your pain because you just know your pain is causing them pain. It causes strain on your social life, on your friends, on your OCD when you have to strike out plans in your perfectly neat diary because you just can't face being out of the house that day (anyone else unable to deal with diary scribbles??..just me??). There is so much more to it than just a few weeks of injections, medications and shoving an egg in at the end of it. This is another reason for wanting to share my journey, to hopefully give some awareness to people who have never been in this situation, people that are ignorant to it, people that just don't understand but want to, people who are just damn lucky enough not to have to learn about it.

Do you know what? Sometimes I sit and wish I was one of those people, "the normal people" as I think of them or "the lucky ones" but then I tell myself NO! you do not want to be one of the them, you are you! and this is your destiny, your journey and you was put on this earth strong enough to deal with it, to fight it, to learn from it, to become the stronger person you are today.

Now as much as I do believe that's how I am, there are days sometimes weeks, where I just can't believe. Every single ounce of me disagrees. Every part of me wants to give up the fight, my head thinks I just can't do this today! I just sit there angry at the world, angry at myself, angry at the doctors & nurses that have done nothing but help me, but I can't help thinking awful things about them, which deep down I do not mean! For instance, the radiographer that scanned me when we went into hospital pregnant for the first ever time with abdomen pain and vomiting, not finding our baby trapped in my tube. Yes, I know it's not a "formed baby" I was only 6 weeks but to me it was our baby and they missed it on the scan. So, I was sent home, my life at risk, our baby in my tube and continued to eat the grapes and banana milkshake I craved. *Ectopic pregnancy symptoms heighten early on, hence cravings at 6 weeks and the biggest boobs I had ever had, at that point anyway.* Angry at the Doctor who told me the following day she was keeping me in overnight as she wanted me to have a laparoscopy the next morning. I remember listening to that Dr shout at the staff outside my room "Who on earth sent this girl home!? Her levels are sky high; she is pregnant and there is fluid on her scan!" Luckily my tube didn't rupture before I had surgery or they would have been in a lot of trouble. Anyone who has met my mother would know there would have been hell to pay.

I still feel angry at the surgeon who told me he not only removed our baby but removed my tube too! I can't remember his name, but I remember his face, and his voice telling me how sorry he was. I'm getting angry just thinking about them which is ridiculous when this is 7years ago now and they were only doing their jobs. But once that dark cloud starts to disperse in your mind, the reality of it all comes flooding back in and you remember the precious moments that happened too.

I remember sitting in the hospital with my mum and my OH (other half) with the doctor who told me she was keeping me in overnight and the look she gave me when I burst out crying because I did not want to stay. "We have a table booked for tea with friends, we can't let them down" Looking around at them hoping one of them could find a reason for me not to stay. I did not want the outcome I knew was coming. She looked at me with the deepest sympathy and love, a stranger who knew nothing about me but knew I was terrified and was there for me in that moment.

I remember my mum holding back tears because she knew, she just knew. (mum's just do don't they)

I remember my OH holding my hand and not letting go. He stayed with me as long as the ward staff would let him that night, he even nipped out to get us a Domino's pizza that the nurse let him sneak in. He was back first thing waiting for me when I came out of surgery. That morning was the first time I had seen him cry a little. He hugged me when I broke down after the surgeon dropped his bombshell and he told me we will be okay. I knew right there and then I would be because I had him.

and I still had my other tube, right????....

xx

"The emerging woman will be Strong minded, Strong hearted, Strong souled and Strong bodied...Strength & Beauty must go together"
Louisa May Alcott

Chapter 2
My OH – Monsieur Gaston

OH, is an abbreviation we use on the infertility forums and chats it stands for Other Half. This chapter is to my other half.

It's probable that he will read my book at some point so let me start off by saying "THANK YOU!"

Thank you for everything. Thank you for standing by me. Thank you for making me laugh when I'm nervous or scared. Thank you for not moving out when I had crazy mood swings. Thank you for cheering me up on the bad days, for smiling with me on the good days. Thank you for being on this hideous journey with me when it's not a path you have to take.

Does anyone else feel a heavy sense of guilt when their OH could quite easily conceive if they were with someone else??

Now obviously deep down I know he wouldn't leave me for not being able to have a baby naturally but it's one of those thoughts that are in the back of my mind and I just feel so guilty. Can't help thinking sometimes, Should I let him go so he can have a family?? He would make an AMAZING daddy and I'm the reason he isn't one. Fatherhood really would be the making of him. He has what we refer to as "super sperm" I think the average sperm count ranges between 15 million to more than 200 sperm per millilitre and he was 121 million so on the higher on the end of the scale. I mean he got me pregnant with two blocked tubes, yes two blocked, not just one but two (cue eye roll).

I told you about our ectopic pregnancy which resulted in me losing one of the blocked tubes, I was advised at this point that my other tube was blocked, and IVF would be our only option, cheers for the good news doc. Well 16months later I was rushed into hospital with severe pains, had some wonderful non-degrading internal scans (there's that eye roll again) and was told I needed another laparoscopy which resulted in them removing my now distended tube that was causing me so much pain and a couple of adhesion's just for added fun. My OH must have thought "For god sake this girl is never out of hospital, what have I got myself into!"

The day after I was discharged from hospital, we had horrific news that one of the most precious people in OH's life had taken ill and was going to hospital. This was the beginning of the most devastating and life changing experience my poor OH has had to go through. It was my turn to support him. *(I am not going into detail on what happened as it's not my story to tell, it's his and I have to respect that)*

Now in any other time I would have completely put our IVF to one side and left it until he was ready, but time was ticking and said loved one wanted more than anything to be a grandparent and I was going to try my hardest to get them a grandchild.

Unfortunately, we ran out of time and I will forever feel like I failed them.

We have been through more sadness in a relationship than people will ever know but to think of how happy we are today just show's me we can handle anything together. He continues to support me, and I will forever continue to support him.

It's very easy to forget about your OH as technically all they have to do is "their business in a pot" which granted cannot be comfortable in a room that resembles a prison cell with a wide range of dirty magazines. But at least their day has a happy ending. Forget is probably the wrong word for it, more like dismiss them. It's by no means intentional, you just spend so much of your energy trying to be strong and get through it that your sucked into the IVF whirlwind and can leave them on the side-lines at times. For that OH I am sorry.

He has been to scan after scan after scan, appointment after appointment after appointment. He puts up with a lot, anyone that knows my OH also knows I do too hehe. The crying (I do this a lot) sometimes happy tears, like when I am half way through stimulation and he brings me a brew in bed and I cry once he has left the room because I am so happy he did something so little but something so thoughtful. All part and parcel of the IVF craziness.

Then there's the sad tears, the crying so hard you can't breathe tears and he sits there silent holding your hand, so you know he is there and keeps his pain to himself. Then there's the shouting along with random silent treatments, because he has done something to annoy you, but you haven't told him because he is just supposed to know what he has done without me telling him. Pretty sure us women do that anyway as a rule, but it definately seems more often during IVF.

There are also the physical changes they deal with. Now I know this shouldn't really be a factor because they love you and are supposed to love you regardless of what you look like. But when your body now resembles Homer Simpson with bruises it is bound to affect them. It offends my eyes never mind his. Obviously, he wouldn't dare mention that to me with the number of hormones that are pumping through my veins.

Can you believe he is going to go through all of it again with me??!!

Chapter 3

How does a moment last forever?

"Sorry but IVF is your only chance to get pregnant...."

Words that will stick with me forever, words that in that moment changed my life forever.

So, at this stage I am living life without fallopian tubes. The left tube taken with our ectopic pregnancy and my right has now been removed due to distension that was close to rupturing. I can no longer conceive naturally.

I don't actually know if I am classed as "Infertile" or not, as my ovaries function just fine. At least at this point they do; we will find out on my next stimulation if not. My uterus lining is just fine, and my cycle is always on time (sings Ashanti Ja-Rule in head) but I physically cannot get my eggs fertilized. His "super sperm" will always come to the end of the road (sings Boyz II men...not sure where these songs are coming from) they will always hit a wall and get no further. I will ovulate but my eggs will never get anywhere. So, I just need to get them from A to B, sounds simple right??...wrong! You will see how wrong I was to think that.

Knowing you can no longer conceive naturally is like being told your no longer useful as a woman, your body can no longer do what it is supposed to do. Your left feeling like you are a constant failure, not only to your OH, your family but to human nature. At least that's how I feel anyway....

Some women don't want children, for some it's just not something they would choose for themselves. Which is fine that's their choice and everyone is entitled to their own life choices. But not me, it is something I have always wanted. For as long as I can remember I have wanted to be a mummy, to have my own baby/babies. Instead I am constantly on the side lines watching others make a family.

Whether its family, friends or a friend of a friend it hurts you to the core knowing it is not you and may never be you. Now don't get me wrong I am always happy for them and would never do anything to taint that happiness, but unfortunately their happiness is my sadness. I would never want them to go through what I go through, what other people that are also on this journey go through. I honestly wouldn't wish it on my worst enemy. But it doesn't stop the resentment, the jealousy, a feeling that's with me every day, the feeling that I may never be a mum. Sounds so self-indulged doesn't it.

But that feeling is with me every day, from the moment I was told IVF was my only option that feeling has lasted and never left. Now although I have this feeling it doesn't mean that I am unhappy in anyway because I'm not. I have the most amazing people surrounding me and I love them dearly. There is absolutely nothing I dislike in my life (other than the obvious...IVF) I have family. I have friends (a handful but they are good ones). I have a career I love. A beautiful home, my OH who I cannot wait to marry and our puppy. She isn't a puppy anymore actually she is 6. We got her a few months after we lost our first baby.

I do get up most days feeling blessed for everything I have, but it is always in the background, that feeling, I am not a mum and may well never be one. I am not sure if it's just me or if other people feel this too, but I am constantly in turmoil with myself. Constantly not really knowing how I am really feeling and finding most emotions quite overwhelming. If I feel true happiness I am reduced to tears, I felt this the night OH asked me to be his wife. I felt it each time I saw "pregnant" or double lines on the home pregnancy tests. I find that when something is sad or painful, I feel numb, because nothing compares to the pain I have felt. Sometimes I feel "normal" and feel sadness and happiness like "normal people"

The world of IVF can be a really lonely place. It's really strange (at least this is my thoughts anyway) because even though you know others are going through the same, some are even going through a worse time, and even though your surrounded by your loved ones the whole way through you can still have moments when you feel completely and utterly alone. (Cue the smallest violin) I have always had quite bad anxiety for a number of different reasons and unfortunately, I over think because of it so I am constantly in my head which is a very lonely place to be.

I am learning to control my thoughts with different techniques, I don't know if you will of heard of a book called "the chimp paradox" but it's brilliant and it really helped me, so basically it's picturing your brain as chimps, I know it sounds ridiculous but it works. So, I have a positive chimp and a negative chimp and when I have negative thoughts I picture said chimps and I get the positive one to have a word with the negative one, sounds crazy I know but it honestly works. A not so crazy technique is exercise, I love to go to the gym it's a real stress reliever for me, running in particular is good for me and I signed up to do the EPT1000. Which is 1000 miles in a year, doesn't seem a lot but it means 20miles a week for a year, it's a lot trust me. Spending time with my OH helps my anxiety, getting dressed up and getting out of the house together works wonders. Alcohol doesn't work, well it does at the time but the next day when that dreaded beer fear kicks (omg awful) my anxiety is just through the roof and I become very lonely in my head again.

The loneliness isn't something I really understand, I don't get why I feel like that. I have so many loved ones around me. I have even made new friends through IVF but something in my mind just doesn't feel right and makes me feel alone. It is hard to explain when I don't understand it myself. I suppose it is just living in my head that causes it (you'd think the chimps would keep me company up there).

Maybe it's because no one else knows how it feels, people that are on a similar journey have an idea of what it feels like because they are on a similar path. But they don't feel what I feel just like I don't feel what they feel. I suppose that goes for anything in life though, not just IVF. No one person feels the same as the next person. People that are not on this journey or similar, try so hard to know what you are feeling. To put themselves in your shoes, to try their upmost to be on your level so they can help you and support you, but they just don't. Don't get me wrong I love and appreciate everything my loved ones say and do for me and the amount of effort they make to be on my level, but they just never will be because they are not me. Which is why I guess it can feel so lonely even when you are not alone, it's like your alone in your head but not in your heart.

Chapter 4

Unwitting Host

"**UNWITTING** *adjective* without knowing or planning, Not expected"

So, as I sit in Cafe Nero having my latte (and a cheeky chocolate pastry) before I go for my bloods and scan I am suddenly overwhelmed with different emotions. Thinking of all the times I have been here before, thinking of my past treatments and of my uncertain future. I nearly cried the moment I got on the motorway at 6am (I put it down to the 5.15 alarm). I really was not expecting to feel like this at all, actually I don't know what I was expecting to feel like but not like this. I am excited to be back because it's one step closer. I am sad because it reminds me of our lost babies. I am nervous about what my next treatment will be like (please be better than the last). And I am terrified of this next Stimulation.

On our first stimulation it started off quite well, other than being a crazy person on my medications. Doing little things like getting in the car to go somewhere and driving half an hour past where you were supposed to be going because you forgot why you was even in the car in the first place. Being in the middle of a conversation then forgetting what you were going to say. Putting the frying pan in the fridge, getting infuriated by the fact it will not fit in the fridge. Then there's the usual tiredness that comes with your medications, the hunger that makes you eat everything in sight. On one round I had a share bag of Jalapeño and cheese max crisps every day and glass of milk with them as they set your mouth on fire. Then there are the emotions, crying for no reason, being so needy to be honest I am pretty needy anyway, but I really out do myself with the neediness when on treatment. The soreness and bruises on your tummy from your injections, so not only can you no longer fit in your jeans from bloating but your skin is too sore for the jeans that do fit (stretchy pants all the way ladies!).

Then comes the stuff you did not expect, the unwitting stuff!!! The type of things that are kind of mentioned briefly as a risk but doesn't happen very often (stats are below).

Once you have started stimulation you are monitored every other day to keep an eye on your levels and scans to check the size of the follicles they are stimulating on your ovaries. Once they are happy with the size of them, they send you for egg collection. We did quite well at our egg collection we got 10 embryos,7 of which fertilized, and 3 was frozen and then on named "Frosties".

The day after egg retrieval I became very out of breath with a belly which looked like I had eaten a small child…whole!!not sure where that reference came from, let me say that again…. with a belly that looked like I was 4months pregnant. I was taken as an emergency to Gynae at RPH and was soon diagnosed with Ovarian Hyper-stimulation Syndrome. There are 3 levels of OHSS, Mild Moderate and Severe. I was moderate. I was sent home to rest and hope that the fluid would subside. There was so much fluid in me that I was so out of breath I could barely get up the stairs, and I waddled like a fat penguin. I then panicked thinking we wasn't going to be able to go for our embryo transfer. So, I rang our clinic in Manchester to inform them what had happened, and they assured me we was still fine to go ahead and it will be put on my notes. But it wasn't put on my notes and no one on the day of transfer was even aware until I said how relieved I was that they went ahead after how poorly I had been. We had a day 5 blastocyst transferred but unfortunately it didn't take and AF (annual flow/aunty flow) arrived halfway through the dreaded 2 weeks wait, which is hardly surprising considering how ill I was. I still wonder if the nurse on the phone had done her job and written my OHSS in my notes whether or not they would have gone ahead. Maybe they would have frozen the embryo I feel like they wasted. Guess we will never know.

A few months later we thought we would try one of our "Frosties", surely a Frozen Embryo Transfer would be easier. Surely less could go wrong this time. NOPE! It was worse.

I started the medications as advised but after a few days I started with really bad headaches and dizziness. So being the serial ringer that I am I rang to tell them about my headaches "just power through" so I powered through for a couple of days, but the headaches got worse and I started with nausea. I rang again. "just power through its quite normal to have some side effects" so powered through again and carried on taking the medications. Then I woke up with blurred vision. It was like I had blinkers on. So... yes you guessed it...I rang again!! I don't remember being the most pleasant of people over the phone (sorry to whoever you were) but I had been telling them I was unwell and now I was at risk of losing my eyesight!! After a few brain scans and blood tests they sent me for a Lumbar Puncture. Now if you have been unfortunate enough to endure one of these you have my deepest sympathy. If you haven't well count yourself lucky.

So, they told me they think the medication had caused my hormones to raise so high that it caused fluid on my brain, Idiopathic Intracranial Hypertension IIH. At the time of the LP I was actually feeling okay, probably the best I had felt for a while, but I had been off the medications a while by this point, so my hormone levels had dropped. They took some fluid out and said I would probably get a really bad headache so severe you actually have to stay horizontal so that your spinal fluid level reaches your brain to reduce the pain of your brain being squished!!!...this headache lasted about a week. I have never known a headache like it, it really was like someone was squishing my brain. The pressure of the fluid has caused permanent damage to the nerve behind my eye. I had my eyes tested only the other week and they can still see the damage (5 years later)

A few weeks later my vision began to improve, and the dizziness started to subside and after a few months I was given the all clear for driving and to return to work. They said I was fine to continue with Fertility treatment, but I was to be monitored closely. As you can imagine after all of this our confidence in the treatment and our clinic was somewhat diminished. This led us to make the decision to have a non-medicated FET (Frozen Embryo Transfer) once we were ready. But my body needed time to heal, we needed to get back to some kind of normality so we took a break so we could feel refreshed for the next round.

MODERATE OHSS 1% that's 1 IN 100 WOMEN

IDIOPATHIC INTRACRANIAL HYPERTENSION is 0.8-1.7 out of 100,000 people

Chapter 5

Forever can spare a minute

So far, our treatment seems to have gone on forever! We have only done one stimulation and one FET which is not a lot but when things go wrong the process becomes twice as long and recovery takes time, mentally and physically. They say time flies when you are having fun, well time freezes when your living hell on earth through IVF.

Those two treatments from start to finish lasted 12months, just two treatments that actually take 6 weeks each, not something we expected to happen I can assure you. After the FET went so horribly wrong, we decided I needed a break, my body was a mess! No embryo in its right mind would want to get comfy in me in that state. And Forever can spare a minute.

From the FET being cancelled due to the fluid on my brain to us ringing to request our first non-medicated FET it was 7months. 5months of that gap was filled with scans, lots of eye tests, lots of appointments, lots of headaches with sickness, lots of crying and a Lumbar Puncture. Once I had recovered and was given the okay to work, the okay to drive and the okay to continue with treatments I focused 2months solely on myself. Going to the gym, running, spending time on my mindset and on just being happy with my OH, family and friends. Eventually I finally felt ready to take on another round, let's get them "Frosties" defrosted!!! (or thawed as the doctors would put it).

We decided only to transfer 1 "Frosty" to start with, the non-medicated rounds are a lot simpler and easier. You go off your own body timings and any symptoms you have are not from medications because you are not on any (thank the lord). The only thing is because you are not on medication, they cannot control what day you are going to ovulate so if it falls on the wrong day it will get cancelled. They don't do any Frozen Embryo transfers on a weekend at my clinic. So, we had a 5-day blastocyst and transfer would be 6days from ovulation. So as long as my body ovulated any other day than a Sunday or Monday, we would be fine for transfer. So, I started POAS (peeing on a stick) from CD10 (cycle day 10) and continued until I saw the smiley face on my test, which was CD15. We were booked in and my lovely little grandad took me for my transfer. He has been unbelievable throughout all my treatments, could not have coped without him. He got up at 5.30am on so many occasions to take me for bloods, scans and transfer day when my OH couldn't get out of work, he is my favourite person, every time we went we listened to Frank Sinatra's Under my skin (I actually have 4 favourite males in my life, my dad, my grandad, my OH and my nephew).

After the transfer I rested for the first 3 days, I did the bed rest some people advise against but some favour it. After 3 days I moved around got fresh air and spent time away for few days with OH's family. I had symptoms from around day 6 on my 2week wait, sore and very large boobs, bloated, hungry, extreme tiredness I had a lot of naps) and I wanted milkshakes which I craved when had our ectopic (strange and very early for cravings I know but nevertheless I wanted it) I started to spot on day 8 and no matter how much I prayed for it to be implantation bleed it wasn't to be and AF arrived with a vengeance. It was the most painful period I have ever had; I couldn't move for the excruciating pain and I have never seen so much blood, up until this point anyway, sorry for being so graphic. I hadn't done an early pregnancy test like I wanted to (a lot of us do on the 2 weeks wait) because I was away I managed to resist. I am pretty convinced that our de-frosty had started to implant around day 5 or 6 but just couldn't get comfy enough to stay. It was classed as unconfirmed miscarriage as I hadn't tested. Any woman will tell you you just know when you are and know when something is wrong. I knew from the first spotting that it wasn't implantation. You just know.

I rang the clinic to tell them what had happened, and they said we could go ahead and try again straight away as there was no medication to get out of my system. So, I began to POAS once again from CD10, here we go, round 4. But it was not meant to be, I ovulated on a Monday (Typical!) so we were cancelled. I was devastated but looking back it will have been for the best. After the pain my body had been through the month before it probably could do with the rest.

We could begin the next round and what a round it was. It ended up being our best and worst round of them all.

Chapter 6

The East Wing

This may just be the hardest chapter for me to write, it is still so very raw and painful for me to think about never mind share with you all, but I promised to write from the heart with complete honesty about the good and the bad parts of my journey. This just so happens to be the good and the bad.

So, our last non-medicated FET was cancelled due to me ovulating on the wrong day, but we were allowed to ring on my next AF which we did. Once again, I was told to start POAS from CD10, this time around I got my smiley face on CD17 and we were booked in for our blastocysts to be transferred 6days later with our last 2 Frosties. Both Frosties thawed successfully on the morning of transfer day so we could set off to get the our Frosties put in so they could start getting comfortable. You have to drink a certain amount of water that morning, they give you a time to start drinking it so it times right with the transfer list so that your bladder is full and they get a good view of your uterus. Well the list was late! I was bursting, like painfully bursting. Don't know if you have ever had to do this but the art of only letting some urine out and keeping the rest in takes some serious concentration. I somehow managed to let just enough out that I didn't wet myself, and when I went in, the doctor between my legs said "My word I have never seen a bladder so full!" she actually had to catheterise me so she could find my uterus. How I did not urinate on that poor doctor I will never know.

When they do the transfer, they pass the Embryos through a little tube from the Embryologist. You get to see this little dot arrive in your lining on the screen. It's not the embryo you can see because that's microscopic, but you can see the glue it's in. It looks like a little shooting star on the screen and they give you a picture to keep. After the transfer I went home to relax, an hour's journey home from Manchester, thinking about my baby shower and how I am going to decorate the nursery, because this is our time.

The first day after transfer I rested, being horizontal as much as possible with my butt raised on a pillow on the couch watching Disney films. Rubbing my belly like a Lucky Buddha. On my 2nd day past transfer (2DP5DT) the sun came out and was quite possibly the hottest day of the year, so I got out the paddling pool and my book (Under rose tainted skies – Louise Gornall. Amazing book) and I sat on the raised bit in the pool so that my butt was out of the water you know just in case I washed the baby out. I sat and ate my brazil nuts, pineapple slice, and drank my Pom Juice relaxing in the sunshine. These are all tips and tricks from the forums I have read. Apparently, they help implantation, OH actually googled things to help and one was keeping my feet warm, so I was ordered to put on my fluffy socks, no arguments from me I love a fluffy sock. It seems to be a thing on forums to also wear socks that have pineapples on or unicorns. More symbols of luck.

I returned to work then from 3DP5DT, I sit at a desk and manage my own work load so I felt it would be better for me to go in and take my mind off it all because the 2ww drives me crazy. The 2-week wait is the time from transfer to being allowed to do your first pregnancy test. Who knew that 2 weeks, just 14days!! could feel like a year?

I had managed to stay sane for 1DP, 2DP, 3&4 DP (days passed) but on 5DP I woke up and thought "I am pregnant" and I just knew it!!!...so I was really naughty and I did a test...

...there they were the most beautiful 2 lines I had ever seen, I was pregnant :)

As you can imagine I burst out crying into happy tears. I'm now just remembering that feeling, this glow from deep inside my tummy just burst happiness through my whole body I had never felt happiness like it!!! It was like magic!!!

I waited all day to tell OH, it killed me not calling or texting but it's not really something I could tell him over the phone. So when he got home from work I told him the wonderful news, he thought I was lying. He couldn't believe it and he couldn't believe I had tested so early, whoopsie. We were over the moon. We were Pregnant!

On Day 6 I decided to test again, just to make sure obviously, they were still there 2 strong lines. This was really happening!! We were having a baby. "Don't get too excited" he said "It's still too early" he said "I won't" I said :) .... whilst sat googling my nursery furniture. Please tell me other people trying to conceive do this and not just me.

I had two strong BFPs (big fat positives) so we decided to tell our family, only immediate family, parents' brothers and sisters. They knew we was having treatment so we couldn't not tell them. I actually told my dad before OH knew which a bit is naughty but also not intentional, but it couldn't be helped he could see it on my face when I got to work, and I did try to lie. "You've not tested yet have you" "Nooooooo of course not" (with huge beaming glow of happiness across my face) he knew straight away. I was busted.

On Day 7 I did another test, again just to make sure BIG MISTAKE!!! One of the lines was lighter than the other, well it was wrong obviously. It was a cheap test, stupid cheap test I told myself. I need a First response test that won't lie to me. So, I got in the car and off I went to Boots and waited outside until the doors opened. OH, was still in bed he had no idea I was even up never mind stood outside a shop at 7.45am. I made my way home and POAS .... two strong lines PHEW!!!!!I knew it was the test that was wrong. First response to the rescue.

Right do not test again until OTD (official test day) just try enjoying it for a bit, so I did. I tried to remain positive and let the days pass knowing I was pregnant. It wasn't easy to do but I somehow managed to get to 13DP for OTD without doing any more tests. If you believe that you will believe anything. I did two tests every day from 7DP-12DP morning and evening. Not told anyone that, feels quite good to get off my chest.

Well 13DP5DT what a day you were. I had saved my expensive digital Clearblue for the special occasion. I got up 6am like I always do and POAS, cue the longest 3mins of my life....

........PREGNANT...... Woooooooooooooo!!!!!!! I'm pregnant, I'm pregnant, I'm pregnant!!!!!!!!

all the hell we had been through to get to this moment was finally over. My OH was going to be a daddy, I was going to be a mummy, my dream had finally come true.

Until 11am when I started to spot (son of a.......!!!)

Around this time my clinic called me to confirm my result, so I told them I was pregnant, but I had just started to spot. They congratulated us and just said to rest up it could just be implantation bleed. As you can imagine the next few hours were awful. Every pee, every wipe checking for blood, every twinge, every cramp. Please Please Please stay comfy in there!!! Please hang on!!!! Around 3pm the cramps got more intense and the spotting was more frequent, so I rang the clinic. They were very sympathetic but there was nothing at this point that they could do. I just had to ride it out and hope it stopped.

10pm I was in A&E (the east wing) because I was just in too much pain and losing too much blood. They asked me to do a urine sample and we had to sit and wait for them to come tell us the result. Our friend actually works there and made sure we were looked after. She left with my sample, but a different doctor came back in the room, I can see his face now, the pure sadness in his eyes as he knew what he was about to tell me was going to break me.

" I'm so sorry...." don't even finish your sentence Doc.

I literally felt my heart break.

OH, looked devastated. He held his head in one hand and my hand in the other and let me cry it out. It was more like screaming than crying. It was the most painful cry I had ever experienced. I can feel the pain now just thinking about it.

"Get this out of my arm, I want to go home" (canula) I was really snappy at the really lovely Dr who had just ruined my life. Then I quickly apologised for my rudeness. I later found out that that lovely Dr cried after he left my room and I was the last patient of his shift, so to that Dr "I am so sorry for ruining your day" (although you did ruin my life...jokes)

I couldn't understand how things had changed so quickly, he said him/her/they was probably hanging on for us but just couldn't stick. He put it in a really reassuring way somehow. But it did change a thing. It was gone.

Nothing could have prepared me for that pain and there are no words to describe it.

So that was it the best and worst day of my life to date. 6am pregnant, 10pm not. It has taken me 6months to consider going back for more treatment and I won't lie I am dreading every second of it. But the support I had through all of the last treatments I know I will get through the next ones. I have the best OH, the best family and the best friends.

So, let's do this, let's try again.

I never met you, but I miss you every day, and I will always wonder who you would have been, forever and always my favourite "what if...?" xx

Chapter 7

"Be our Guest"

Sending invites to events that are either pregnancy related or involves kids...you "normal people" really can't win on this one I'm afraid. Let me explain...

If you send me an invite to your baby shower I am going to be devastated. "Why would you be devastated???" I hear you say, well its simple.... I may never be able to have my own baby shower. I have so many visions in my head of what my Disney inspired baby shower would look like, who I would (and would not) invite to it. What I would wear, in my head I would look very elegant and be "blooming" however I am sure the reality would be very different. What my cake would look like, the games we would play etc etc. This goes for your child's christening, your second child's christening (even worse cos you have more than one child...don't even go there if you have had a third). Same goes for birthdays. Then there's Halloween, World Book Day, Easter and Christmas. The list goes on.

Now before you judge me and think I am just an ungrateful and bitter, that feeling of devastation lasts for a measly few seconds before I am unbelievably happy for you and your little bundle of joy and I'm writing the event in my diary, planning my outfit and choosing your presents online.

It's the same when you see people posting pics of their first scan..."we are so happy to announce that our family of 3 is now a family of 4". My immediate thought is "FFS" again this lasts a matter of seconds before I am so happy for you and literally could burst with happiness that it was so easy for you and you didn't have to go through this hell I am going through. This week alone I have seen 15 pregnancy announcements 15!!! It makes me so happy for all of those 15 but makes me sad inside 15 times over, it sounds selfish and ridiculous I know but it's the reality and craziness of IVF.

But if you didn't invite me, I would be devastated, see why you can't win. Why would you not invite me??...I'm not a leper, I'm not evil and going to think bad of you for inviting me cos I don't have kids or can't have them as the case seems to be. I'm not that miserable and self-absorbed that I wouldn't want to share and be involved in your baby happiness. In fact, I think not being invited would probably feel worse to being invited. But either way there is always that negative spin on everything for me that involves children. It doesn't even have to be an invite to an event, it can be something like moaning you had to get up hungover to your children, or you had a sleepless night because your baby woke you a few times in the night. Complaining about your pregnancy symptoms, be grateful that you have this amazing gift. I am damn sure that I will moan too if it ever happens though. Like I said you can't win. Now as happy as I am that I got a lie in and peaceful day to recover from all the gin (bottle of) and as happy as I am that I got a 10hour solid sleep, it also hurts to the core at times. I don't have a baby to disturb my sleep or torture me when I am hungover, to snuggle me whilst watching a film on the couch regretting all the gins (bottle of). There is just always this negative spin on everything.

It is a constant battle in my own mind of negative thoughts and positive thoughts. Accepting the negative thoughts but overriding them with the positive ones. It is just part of the journey. This afternoon I wrapped my friends baby shower gifts thinking "I hope one day I get gifts like this" "I hope one day I have a baby shower" with that sickening feeling in my stomach telling me that it may never happen for me. But I accepted the negative thought rather than ignoring it and thought "My friend is going to love these gifts at her shower", "I'm so happy for her and her hubby" and I can't wait to meet their little bundle.

In reality I suppose I get all the good bits of kids, because I can borrow other peoples. I can take them to the park when I want to go, not when they are being annoying, and you want to get them out of the house. I don't need to change my hours to suit the school run or stand in the playground cold with all the other mums gossiping. I don't need to attend kids' parties on a Sunday, in a play centre that stinks of sweaty feet and is so loud you come out with your ears buzzing. No dirty nappies. No toddler snot, I actually cannot cope with that. So, I guess I should count my lucky stars really.

For now, I will just have to keep 'borrowing' my nieces and nephew and my godson, and any other baby I see at events. I actually sat for about half an hour, maybe longer, with a baby at the last christening I went to. The mum of the baby knows me quite well but the dad had no clue who I was, he thought I was a complete nutter when I passed him his baby back "I best give you him back before I steal him" the look on his face was a picture. Luckily the mum reassured him she knew me. Sorry just a nutter who wants kids and can't, shouldn't laugh really but if you don't you will cry.

Chapter 8

Saved by the Beast

Have you figured out the theme to my chapter titles?

They are the titles of each chapter of Beauty & the Beast and have somehow been very fitting to my story so far. It is my favourite film and each chapter of the film has linked to each chapter of my story....and IVF is a beast!!!

In the film this chapter "saved by the beast" is where Belle has run off and the wolves try to get her and Beast saves her. I have never been chased by wolves so that is not what this is about :) but I have been saved, Saved in so many ways by so many different people.

It is not always the obvious people like your OH or your family and friends. I have been saved by strangers, by people I have met in waiting rooms, by people I have spoken to over social media in groups for people going through a similar journey to me and they will never really know that they saved me.

For example on a bad day, the days when your keeping all your negative thoughts inside so you post in the group "has anyone ever felt like a complete failure and wanted to give up" and a complete stranger in fact a few of them comment to tell you they have. That instantly saves you from feeling like you're the only person who has every felt that way. You now no longer feel as alone as you did. Writing in Forums on your 2ww "anyone else wanted to test as soon as they got home from egg transfer??" and they will write saying they felt exactly the same and they actually did test just to check!!!! Brilliant!!! saved again. I cannot thank the ladies/gents in these groups enough for sharing their crazy times and thoughts, they don't realise just how much of an impact they have on someone, on me.

I cannot thank my OH and my family enough either, they all try so hard to understand everything, researching and talking to others about their experiences so they can pass it on to me. Reassuring me with positive quotes and advice. Listening to me when I am moaning about it all, laughing with me when I joke about it all, just being there for me through every emotion.

I think for parents it must be so unbelievably difficult for them to watch their child chasing their dream of becoming a parent themselves and they may never achieve it. Mine seem to have quite different views on treatments and solutions but both just want us to be happy. They have been my absolute rocks throughout.

My younger sister/best friend Sarah has been incredible to say the least. I remember her being at my house after a failed round and I was flapping about trying to act like I was fine, and I quite clearly wasn't. She just sat and held me whilst I cried on the floor. She booked a trip away for me and OH so we could see that life without children can be just as good and to give us a bit of happiness after awful news. She had booked us in to a glamping pod, it was brilliant! We walked into the village drank too much and watched England in the world cup. We sat in the outdoor hot tub, made our first fire (with the help of a phone call from a friend) and we laughed together for the first time in weeks. She has been there for me on all my bad days (the ones I told her about) She has sent gifts, inspirational quotes, advice from others because they have confided in her about their journey. I wouldn't have survived without her.

I won't sit and name every friend that has been there for me, but you girls know who you are and I love you.

I won't sit and name the people who have said inappropriate comments or made me feel worthless as it's not worth the time or energy hating on mindless comments like those. I am sure many of you on similar journeys have had the same and a lot of the time it isn't intentional. It's all just part and parcel of infertility, I guess.

So, thank you to everyone that has saved me so far on my beastly journey. Pretty please stick around for the parts still to come because I will need you.

"Through what feels like an eternity of drowning, you all teach me to breathe"

Chapter 9

"Days in the sun"

Do you ever feel like you only get a certain amount of happy days in a row??

You sit there at work thinking you feel blissfully happy, your home life is amazing, you're in love, your friends are true friends, your family are happy safe and well, you love your job. Then all of a sudden you get a tiny thought that completely ruins it.

Remembering tiny details that have such a huge effect.

"I would have started maternity leave this week"

In a few weeks our baby would have been due. By the end of my 30th year I would have been a mum.

Unfortunately, as you know from earlier chapters this was not meant to be. I mean it is partly my own fault for remembering these dates because I get carried away thinking about things before, they even happen. My next treatment hasn't even started and I know that I will be due between Christmas and new year if it's one baby, November if its twins, October if its triplets (omg watch me be the next octo mum) Now I didn't sit there counting the weeks in my diary (have done before now though) I used an IVF calculator online. Yes, that is a real thing you can actually type in the date of your impending embryo transfer in and it will tell you when your due. It will even change it for Donor embryos, frozen embryos and fresh ones.

I'm going to sound even crazier now because I actually haven't even been accepted for my next treatment. But our consultation to discuss getting our next batch of eggs is coming up in a few weeks, 2 weeks before our baby was due and my AF will be due the week of my due date which also happens to be my birthday, if my cycle is bob on time.

Let's hope we get accepted for the next treatment this cycle, try again for our little family. Need to be positive and hold on to the thought that I will get my days in the sun so to speak.

"Days in the sun will return, we must believe as others do, that days in the sun will come shining through."

Chapter 10

"There may be something there that wasn't there before...."

...positive vibes.

Usually walking into the IVF clinic, I feel nothing but bad vibes.

I feel unbelievably nervous, anxious and full of dread. But for some reason this time around I feel really positive.

We are seeing our consultant to discuss our second stimulation and we have decided it will be my last stimulation. It's too much for my body all these injections so this is the last stim for me. Let's hope we get a good batch of eggs to work with, cross everything please.

I actually feel really good about this round which is something I've not felt before so let's hope that's a good sign

Well we couldn't be happier with what he has planned for us. I went in thinking I really want a scratch this time round, not sure why I would want this unpleasant experience, but it could help and he offered me it before I even asked. Brilliant!

I had also read somewhere that a long protocol is better for people with endometriosis and that's the protocol he has suggested for us so I'm really happy.

I have never set foot in the clinic and felt positive, but this time felt so different I felt like I was meant to be there, I felt settled. I felt confident and positive about the next part of our journey. I sat in the waiting room thinking about all our past experiences with IVF, the ups and downs (mainly downs) and how much pain I've been through and do I have the strength to go through it again. I looked at my OH and he smiled at me (people that know him no this is a rare act for his face...only joking if your reading this) and I just knew that I could do this with him by my side.

I'm going to go into this with a positive mind and go with the flow. Not going to over think it like I usually do with everything. I'm going to find my inner warrior and go for it. This is my last stimulation and our last batch of eggs, just so happened to be Easter how very apt. I will give it everything I have to be as relaxed and happy through this process and not dwell on what has gone wrong in the past. This is a new round and I feel so much stronger now than I have done. Even though my endometriosis is trying to beat me down, I'm going to pick myself right back up (once the pain has lifted) keep getting fit, eating right, laughing with friends and family and enjoying life with everyone I love and staying away from the ones I don't.

I rang for my scratch and for my injection teach so within a few days hopefully we would have the date for those, and we can get started.

And so it starts again.... the excitement the fear the nerves the butterflies the anxiety the happy thoughts the emotional turmoil...the start of the next round!!

We got the date for our injection teach a week later and I was told I could have my scratch next month ready to start my meds in the May. Ooooooh I couldn't bloody wait for those injections, sore tummy, bloated tummy, swollen boobs (ok that bit is quite good because at least they are perky for a while) weight gain, hormonal crazy antics. But it's the last stimulation so bring it on. What is the worst that could happen right?

IVF Blog extract:

Why does IVF make me so crazy?? Crazy thoughts. Crazy dreams. Crazy emotions. Crazy, Crazy, Crazy!! Feel like my brain is spinning in my head, heart twisting in my chest, stomach flipping!! I haven't even started my medication yet and I already feel miserable. I wanted to feel different this time round and be positive all the way through but the closer I get to starting the worse I'm getting. There are just too many things to consider, too many what ifs.

What if I don't get any eggs?

What if I get some eggs but they don't fertilise??

What if they fertilise but don't grow?!!

What if they grow but don't grow to day5 blastocysts and can't be frozen?!!

How can I be positive when I have this going round and round in my brain!

Maybe I should just try focus on it day by day and stop forward thinking. But I feel like if I don't think about the what ifs then I'm being unrealistic. I can't just sit here thinking it is all going to be fine it's all going to go to plan when I know full well it probably won't and I'm setting myself up for disappointment. Sometimes it's better to think the worst then anything better than that is good. But then I don't want to be a negative Nora either. But positive Polly just isn't realistic or even possible today.

I need to find something to do daily to work on myself...

1.Exercise and better foods

2. Rest (but too much rest allows me to over think)

3. Read a book

4. Meditation

5. Adult colouring books are quite therapeutic

What do you do to relax, calm your anxiety, distract your mind??

Please help my troubled mind

So for the Injection Teach we both have to attend. We have to get up so early to beat the traffic otherwise the 1hour journey ends up nearly 3. We arrive early and go for a coffee in Café Nero. My OH hates to be early for anything but I love it. I would rather be hours early than a few minutes late. It's the same with any appointment and I am pretty bad for it at the airport too. No bags to check in, checked in online but I will still arrive 2hours before the flight so I can sit have a pint with breakfast, obligatory isn't it?? Buy sucky sweets and do a puzzle.

At the teach we was with another 2 couples, all 3 of us was on different protocols and all different ages. I wonder if theirs worked?? I hope so. So the nurse gives you your booklet and talks you through how to do your injections and what days you need to do everything on and when you will have to come in for bloods and scans. You leave completely mind boggled. It's a good job they give you the booklet to take home because within seconds of leaving the meeting room I had forgot what they had said and this was my second time so would think I would remember some bits, but this was a different protocol so that's my excuse.

Has anyone experienced Phantom pregnancy before their treatment??

I woke up looking 3/4 months pregnant. Massive boobies, huge bump (which I actually love) craving banana milkshake like I did with my ectopic pregnancy. I did the exact same thing on my last stimulation and I didn't really think much of it, but it's happened again, and I've not started my injections yet and I'm not due a bleed for another 3weeks

I researched it and it's quite a common thing for someone with infertility, the longing for a baby and wanting it so badly that your mind convinces your body it's pregnant. I do treat myself as pregnant from the moment I'm accepted for treatment so I guess that contributes as well because I'm obviously not drinking and I'm avoiding foods I would avoid if pregnant.

As cute as my little bump looked it was a kind of "look at what you could have won" moment. Its nearly time to get this show on the road so let's hope that this tummy goes down before I start injections or I'm going to look a right beast! Lets do this.....

Chapter 11

Brave

"Come on you can do this"
"You have got this"
"You are strong, you are brave, you deserve this"

This was on repeat in my mind the whole journey on the morning treatment started. A 5am alarm and a hideous motorway journey which always ends up bumper to bumper (hate the motorway) and I had to change my usual route which was the first challenge of the day but I made there on my own and without having a panic attack, not gonna lie I was pretty proud of myself. I am such a bad motorway driver, actually that's not true. I am great in the day when its quiet and its dry. Get me on there in the rain and my legs go to jelly and I have had panic attacks that make my head go funny and black. Not the greatest thing to happen when driving. But I made it there safe and sound.

I sit in the car doing my makeup because there was no way I was doing it at 5am. I always park in the same carpark and usually in the same parking spot, unless someone has beat me to it. On this occasion I got my spot. Café Nero doesn't open until 7am so I have to wait in the car until then. I make my way round, passing the same drunk lady that sits outside the café each time I have been. I do prefer a Costa or Starbucks to be honest but it has become a tradition at this point to go in Nero for a Decaf Latte and Pain au raisin and my loyalty card stamped. 10 stamps you get a free coffee.

You have to be at the hospital early as possible to try beat the bloods queue. I got there 7.45 and still managed to be 5th in the queue but it's not a problem this time as I as stuck there until 2pm for another appointment.....My endometrial scratch! Luckily for me it was a beautiful day and there is a lovely park across the road so I could go sit there all day with my book and try relax.

Bloods done! Now for the long wait....

I sit in the park writing out my plans for my 2 week wait. Plan in some treats along the way for each hurdle of the treatment. End of down reg, end of stimulation, egg retrieval, transfer etc. Only simple things like, a Cinema date, Chinese Takeaway, Facemask, new shoes. Shoes are an issue for me, issue being I can't stop buying them and never wear them. Anyone else like this?

Something I have learnt from my last cycles is that I need to be distracted. IVF is not running my life this time around. I'm going to continue my life as normally as possible and use my planned distractions to keep me going and keep my positive. I am feeling BRAVE and STRONG this time and I want to keep that feeling throughout. Obviously, I will have my bad days which is completely normal but rather than dwell on the bad I will let myself have that day and pick myself up the next.

It's a hard journey but something just felt so different this time around. Casper (my phantom pregnancy baby) is still in full force, hoping this is my body's way of preparing itself for the real thing

" We are STRONG we are FIERCE we are BADASS we are BRAVE we are WOMEN IN INFERTILITY "

After sitting in the park planning my life, reading my book and going for some lunch, 6hours later it was time to go for my scratch. I had had some mixed comments about the scratch. Some said it was painful and some said they hardly felt it. I'm not joking I was not prepared for what was about to happen to me. The nurses and doctor were very nice and very reassuring, I was fairly comfortable, well as comfortable as you can be with a clamp between your legs and a doctors head peeping at you from down there. "ok ready? Sharp scratch" SHARP SCRATCH! I shot up the bed, the nurse had to grab me so I didn't move any further as the doc was still doing her thing down there. Sharp scratch my eye!! Was like a scalpel cutting my insides out, ok that might be an exaggeration, but it bloody well hurt.

I left all shaky and stressed which is not ideal when you have a long drive home. But that was the trip done with many more to come. Tomorrow, Medication and Down regulation begins.

I was put on Buserelin Injections, for the first few days I felt ok really. I had sore boobs, felt tired and dizzy and was extremely thirsty all the time. I wanted to keep moving this time and still go to gym classes. I managed the odd weights class, but I mainly did half an hour spin classes before work, I found it really helped my mindset throughout. I had bad indigestion through the night and also very real and very scary nightmares. I had one where someone removed my sister's skin and whilst I was stapling it back on she was just laughing, erm this isn't a funny situation Sarah!! I got chased down a corridor that looked the shinning, eaten by sharks, swung on giant chandeliers suspended above a castle and I fell off! How weird do you think I am right now??

Day 6 of the down regulation and the bloating and tiredness was in full force. I looked like a worn out whale. I even had to buy new bras because the boobs and back fat are just out of control. This was definitely my worst day so far! Had a really bad night sleep with more nightmares, felt better after getting dressed up to go for some lunch but came back and had a bit of a weird turn. Suddenly felt all fluey. Nap needed. Cramps and spotting started but that's good because means my bleed is on its way so the meds are working the way they should.

One more week on Buserelin then it is time for bloods to see about starting my stims. Still feeling very positive at this point and just taking each day as it comes and listening to my body. If it wanted rest it got rest, if it wanted food it got food, stretchy pants at the ready.

The following week I suffered with headaches and nausea but I still managed to keep moving and go to come classes, walked Nicky Nook with OH, Williamsons park with my bestie Jade. I had a few bad days with my endometriosis. To anyone that suffers with Endo my heart goes out to you. Other than heartache, Endo is the most pain I think I have ever felt and I have this pain every month. It really is like someone has hold of your ovaries and is squeezing them. Or like your womb is wrapped in barbed wire. Just awful.

So Day 16 of down regulation and I had to go for bloods to see if I was ok to start Stimulation and the results were spot on so we could begin the next stage. Being a completely hideous girlfriend to live with with all these hormones OH decided to treat me to a meal out at the Fenwick arms to cheer me up, also giving him some peace whilst I stuffed my face with good food. He knows the way to my heart, through my stomach.

This round I said to myself I would take it day by day and not worry about things that haven't happened yet and cause myself unnecessary stress worry and massive anxiety attacks like last time.

And do you know what it was working!!

I was the calmest I have ever been on any cycle and this is my 6th. I just focused on getting through each day. I would wake up so moody so I just had to think right stay quiet and calm until it passes have your brew (decaf disappointment) and get ready for work, then set a time to have breakfast and my next brew, that gets me to 11am ish then focus on getting to dinner 12.30 afternoon brew & biscuit 2.30/3 home time 4.30...then plan my evening, listen to your body if it's tired out just lay on the couch and watch the soaps. If it want's fresh air, then go for a walk or sit in the garden with a book. Make sure I had a nice tea, straight after I was showered and settled ready for bed I would have to try get comfy and sleep, although I wasn't sleeping well I loved bedtime because it meant I had made it through another day. Annnnd then repeat all over again.

My symptoms were different everyday so doing it day by day is so much better. I would wake up with headaches and usually I would be like "oh great that's it headaches for 4wks" but this time I was like "right let's rest and sleep it off it might be gone when wake up"

I started my Menopur injections a day earlier than I thought so all the dates I had in my head had all been brought forward a day!!

Had a bit of a meltdown during stims with my hormones, I just started crying out of nowhere and couldn't make it stop. To be honest I am a bit of a crier anyway, my friends will tell you just how pathetic I am with the crying. Happy and sad tears. Getting out of the house and getting some air really helped me mentally, I went for a lovely walk with a friend and her beautiful daughter who just so happens to be an IVF miracle herself. A real life rainbow baby.

Body update: STILL FAT it's now evenly spread which draws the attention away from my belly I suppose but it's on my arms thighs back face boobs ass everywhere!! Tired on and off because still not sleeping through and have a headache.

Once you start stims you have to go in for bloods every other day to check your levels and every other bloods appointment you have to go for a scan to check the size of your follicles and this exhausting process of 5am alarms and drives to Manchester goes on for a week or two depending on how well your follicles are growing. There is a chart that has a green band in and you want as many follicles in that band as you can before they tell you to do a trigger shot. On day 23 of Buserelin and Day 11 of Menopur I got given my date and time for the big trigger shot. Massive needle! This is not a needle you want to have to stab yourself with. On the day of trigger my ovaries were so heavy, they felt like the balloons that hold the "UP" house up hardly surprising when your follicles are 15mm in size each and you have about 40 of them growing. Trigger was booked for 11pm and 36hours later would be going for Egg Collection....Happy Easter.

Chapter 12

Frozen

Well it's egg collection day!! I am led on the hospital bed waiting. OH has gone to do his thing in pot (come on swimmers!) I'm just led here waiting for lady number 2 to go down for her procedure before I get changed into the lovely backless gown they have provided, my extra stone heavier body hanging out of that is not attractive I can tell you.

Made the mistake of weighing myself and I went from 63.5kg/9.10 to 68.5kg/10.7!!!! Thank you injections, thank you very much, no wonder my jeans don't fit.

Have not felt nervous up until this point but it is creeping in now. All the questions and what ifs!

What if his swimmers decide to just paddle today and not front crawl?

What if the follicles on my ovaries are just fluid and no embryos in them?

What if my embryos (if get some) don't like his paddling swimmers!!!??!!

But what if and this is a big what if.... what if his swimmers swam like Olympians winning gold and all my embryos like his Olympic gold medallists!!

What if we get loads!?

Just have to wait and see won't we....

WE GOT 17 EMBRYOS!!!

What a good start.

Now we just had to wait for his swimmers to do their job. SWIM SPERM SWIM!

The next day they rang with our results. How many babies did I have? Yes I know they're not babies but to me they are. To me they are my potential screaming toddler.

 "Out of the 17 embryos 8 fertilised" so your telling me over half have gone. Brilliant.

Now we waited to see how many would survive. They will call to keep us updated. We needed some of them to make it to day 5 then they could be frozen and saved for another round if this one didn't work.

Day 5 they ring, it's the longest wait that morning. So many emotions.

Nervous: I was so nervous for the call to tell me how many of our 8 embryos we still had!

Shocked: was a bit of shock for the embryologist's words to be we have 1 good quality embryo (ermm what about the rest!!!)

Relief: what a relief when she followed that bombshell with you have 1 we are able to freeze today and the other 6 we are going to watch until tomorrow

Annoyed: that they are just going to transfer 1. Erm no you can put two in thanks and not just waste my embryos and risk them not being able to be frozen!!

Accomplished: when she agreed with me and I got my own way, 2 embryos being transferred today

Disappointment: we started off with 17, out of them we got 8, out of them only 1 being frozen and 2 transferred! 17 down to 3!

Grateful: I soon came to realise that actually I should be grateful for the amount I have because so many don't achieve that and let's face it it only takes one!! (Well it should only take one, I have been through 5 so far)

Happy: it's transfer day!!! And in an hours' time I will be PUPO. (Pregnant until proven otherwise) And I am going to enjoy it. I am going to be happy in my little PUPO bubble for the next 2 weeks. So please pray for us, hope for us, send us baby dust, cross your fingers toes and eyes for us.

Bring on the 2 week wait

Chapter 13

Tangled

So over the first 8 days of the 2 week wait I had no spotting at all which is a good sign. But also, a bad one because I haven't had an implantation bleed which I've had on previous cycles. I've put on weight because I can't stop eating. I am literally hungry all the time. My OH has actually told me to stop eating. I am cramping like crazy every single day. I'm sore and achy like you get when u have the flu. I had night sweats so bad I would have to get in the shower and the nightmares continued.

Mentally I have only really felt mental from8 days past transfer which is late on for me, I'm usually testing and googling from 2dp not 8. So I'm doing good this time round, but my anxiety is slowly creeping up on me the closer test day gets....but another day ticked off just 4 full days to get through to find out if these two little eggs have stuck!!

Days 8-12DPT My symptoms all started to change. I was so tired. My sense of smell was insane. I had nausea. Cramps on and off. My dog Bella was acting bizarre, she knows when something changes. I swear I know when I have implanted because of her. So on 10dpt I tested. There they were those beautiful blue lines, a nice strong BFP (big fat positive)

And like clockwork I started spotting.

OFFICIAL TEST DAY. Gosh what a day of emotions. Really have been tangled up with myself. So OTD has finally arrived and what a drama. I woke up 4am and did my Clearblue digital (won't be using them again) it said the dreaded words "not pregnant" I felt sick but was like "I'm not having that!"

I got dressed, got in my car at 4.15am and set off to Asda to buy some reliable tests because this one was clearly broken.

One clear blue normal not digital and a trusty first response

Then I drove my loony self-home. I got back in bed and led there until it had been 2hrs since my last wee (longest wait ever) oh and once again whilst I was doing all of this my OH is completely unaware I have tested or been to ASDA as I didn't want to wake him and worry him. So once my bladder had filled up off I went with my tests, 3mins later (felt like 3hrs) clear blue showed faint positive and first response showed a stronger but still faint positive. Both on my second wee of the day but I couldn't get my head around all the tests looking so different!!

Clear blue digital: no

Clear blue normal: maybe

First response: yes

How does that even happen!!! 3 tests 3 outcomes

So I prayed to our embryos, prayed to lost loved ones, prayed to god and waited for the clinic to ring. 10.30 they ring, and made the decision that I must test again the next day (great 24hrs of hell)

It all felt very strange, part of me was excited because you can't get a false positive, part of me was still devastated at the sight of "not pregnant" I was confused at the maybe, and then bring in the what ifs. What if I'm pregnant but I'm losing it that's why it's faint, what if I'm just pregnant and this is my time (that's a good what if) what if it's a chemical pregnancy? What if what if what if what if!! Exhausting!!!

I tried to spend my day thinking positive and think well at the minute they are still in there because my HCG level showed on a test so they haven't gone yet. And they may not go, so let's focus on that. Let's focus on the light at the end of this very long dark tunnel... focus on the dream... focus on the happy ever after.

Once again our fairy tale ending wasn't meant to be. AF arrived. We had lost our baby/babies.

I am still convinced to this day that they both stuck, which is why I got such a strong positive early on. But for some reason my body would not accept them and could not keep them safe. The fight continues.

"I won't stop, for every minute of the rest of my life, I will fight" Rapunzel, Tangled

Chapter14

"A girl worth fighting for"

Well it was time to get on with life again, time to pick ourselves back up and be "normal" for a while. Not the IVF couple. So we enjoyed what was left of summer. Drank too much, Ate too much. Didn't really matter as I resembled a whale anyway. We spent time with our friends and family.

We had a holiday booked for September. 10days in Lanzarote at H10 Rubicon Palace. This was booked before we did our last treatment, I had planned to do a "bikini bump pic" ready for us to announce our baby/babies to everyone once we made it to 12weeks. Just like the beautiful Rosie Huntington whitely did, obviously my pic would be just like hers, I wish.

There are so many thoughts that go through your mind when you have too much time to think, when you give yourself the chance to reflect on it all.

One: How amazing is it being on holiday without kids!!! Literally my only worries for the day are what time should I eat what time is it socially ok to have my first beer (11am onwards is the answer) and which side of my body should I tan (the body IVF has ruined) I lie by the pool and think WOW holidaying with a child looks awful, they cry they scream they wonder off they spill food spill drinks they walk off towards the pool without armbands on...they are whirlwinds and it looks exhausting!!

Two: How amazing would it be to be on holiday with our own kid!!! When the little whirlwinds smile at their mummy n daddy and you can hear them laughing and you can see them all just making memories, me and my OH laughing and smiling cos someone else's kid did something cute. That heart wrenching feeling of "I may never have one of those"

Three: It doesn't matter if we have kids or we don't have kids we are happy being on holiday with my OH just reminds me of how much we love each other and how much we have grown together. How different we are now to when we first met. The scars we now carry on our hearts. IVF takes a toll on a relationship, it's not easy to survive it. But so far, we are doing good. Obviously, we have argued as much as the rest of people, it would be weird if we didn't. But no matter what so far, we have managed to get through it all together and come out stronger.

For the first time in forever I am sat by the pool happy and content, I'm not worrying about my size (I'm not fat but I'm bigger than my usual) I'm not worried about what other people think, I'm just being me. I have really had to fight hard with myself about my body confidence, every single round has ruined my body in some way or another. Whether it's been internal or external the changes are there. And I'm finally coming to terms with the fact that those changes are out of my control. I can diet I can exercise, and I can be as healthy as possible, but those hormones are going to change it regardless.

Every round I have to pick myself up mentally, have to start from scratch and build myself back up to happy. And every round I have to build myself up physically. This last round I gained 1.5stone!! A friend said "it's 1.5stone of sexy" what an amazing way to look at it. Thanks Jayne.

Ladies that have had a baby don't beat themselves up about their weight gain cos they have had a baby so at least they gained something out of it, a couple of stone and a beautiful baby or two, I just gain weight, heartache and have to start again. Now unfortunately I am one of those ppl that are really hard on themselves and get really upset when I don't look the way I want to, so I change myself, tattoos, diets, filler & Botox, hair colour, a shitload of squats. But it makes me feel better about myself. I enjoy making the changes that are in my control because I have no control over anything else.

A lot of people won't like it, but I do and so does my OH so what harm is it doing??

My Body My Choices My life, it is just me being me. I embrace the changes I make myself just like I'm having to embrace my scars from surgery's, my stretch marks from pregnancy's I have lost, big boobs from meds and pregnancies, cellulite from my last round, darker thread veins in my legs from last round, pigmentations from medication and so much more.

Learn to love your body, love yourself, love your scars, embrace it all, embrace your journey and what your body has been through and be proud of yourself and your body

"Beauty is the opposite of perfection - it's about confidence charisma and character"

Chapter 15

Days

Some days I really struggle

Some days I don't want this life

Some days I don't want to be on this journey

Some days I cry

Some days I hurt inside

Some days I just sit and think of our angel babies

Most days I dream of our rainbow baby

Most days I am grateful for being strong enough for this journey

Most days I am happy

Most days I dream that it will all be worth the pain because someday we will have our baby

Every day is different

Every day is a day closer to our dream

Every day is a blessing to be healthy and have a healthy family and be loved

Chapter 16

"Hellfire"

The anxiety has been overwhelming, overpowering and just exhausting. Spending days so unsettled and battling with myself, so many thoughts, fears and emotions my body just can't decide which to deal with first.

Sat here again in Cafe Nero collecting my stamps before I go for some bloods, sat with a caramel latte and gingerbread man. Thinking of Christmas, thinking how I could be 11weeks pregnant this Christmas if round 8 works (would have been 30weeks if round 6 hadn't gone so horribly wrong at 6weeks) or I could be normal and just eating Stilton wheels and drinking Baileys coffees daily. We shall see

Round 7 was a non-medicated frozen round but I surged on the wrong day to be accepted for transfer so it was cancelled. Surge means the day you ovulate, you levels surge, you get a smiley face on an ovulation stick and if it happens on the wrong day of the week and your transfer lands on a weekend they won't do it. So we go to round 8.

Round 8!! Who would have thought in April 2016 on our first round we would be still doing this in October 2018. It's so crazy to realise how much of my life so far has been full of heartache, mainly to do with trying to be a mummy (other things too but I won't bore you with that)

Now don't get me wrong I have had some absolutely amazing times and I have sooooo many happy memories with OH family and friends. I have a really happy life! And I certainly wouldn't ever class myself as "unhappy" without a baby but it's always there...that feeling...that emptiness...that purpose in life that I'm missing...that feeling of loss and mourning for all the babies we have lost on this journey (5!) Grieving for the life we could have.

It's different to losing a baby normally I think (just my personal opinion) for people that miscarry when conceived naturally it's already a baby, for me if I don't make it passed OTD then I lose an embryo. It's not a baby yet but in my mind it's still a baby because it's our embryo but it's not a baby yet (confusing to read never mind feel) Ectopic baby loss, it's a baby it's a miscarriage, it's life changing because they take some of your chance to conceive naturally away from you (your tubes) then there's the embryos that stick but are yet to get passed 6 weeks, they are babies already they are attached. People say well it's better to lose it earlier on, is it??!! I don't know. It didn't feel better to me at OTD or 5weeks or 6weeks or 8week ectopic. They are all just as painful and heart breaking as the last one.

But I need to try not dwell on all the loss. I need to try focus on the next round, this round! Need to keep positive (easier said than done) I need to think and manifest some good into my life (fertility life, I'm happy with rest of my life) maybe if I picture myself at 11weeks at Christmas, if I picture it often enough and pray hard enough it will happen.

So here we go, round 8.

So I am on day 8 of my blood tests to check my LH levels and waiting for my surge! Day 15 of my cycle. This time around I wasn't allowed to do the home ovulation tests so I had to travel in every day to have a blood test.

The clinic called me to say "you've surged" and booked us in for my transfer next week. We were so happy to be booked in and I was so relieved to not be travelling in every day.

The clinic rang again "I'm really sorry I gave u the wrong result" are you kidding me!!!!

How on earth does that even happen. The incompetence of this clinic is just unbelievable. The only reason they realised their error was because whilst I was wittering on on the phone to them I said "oh that's early in my cycle for me" I witter when nervous, also laugh n smile which is usually highly inappropriate. So when she got off the phone she double checked as I had said it was early for me, good job checked because wasn't my result. So we are no longer booked in for transfer, hopes raised then crashed bk down. I would have to continue going in for bloods. Only have one last day to surge or it will land on a weekend and we will get cancelled again. Guess what happened, that's right you guessed it, surged on the wrong day. They accepted us for treatment to start again on my next cycle in a few weeks.

We did just that, I called them on Day 1 of my cycle and I was told to start my ovulation sticks from Day 8. This time they were letting me do the tests at home. Day 7 arrives the day before I am about to start and I get a call from the clinic....

"Good morning Miss Taylor I'm really sorry to tell you but you're not accepted for treatment this month but you can try again on your next cycle"

HELLFIRE!!This clinic is something else.

"We have already been accepted for treatment. I am starting testing from tomorrow"

"No you haven't been accepted we are full this month"

Oh right I must be making it up then. Must have been a figment of my imagination the member of staff telling me we had been accepted and to start testing on day 8 of my cycle.

That was it. I was done with this place. We weren't going to set foot in that building again.

And we didn't.

Chapter 17

"How far I'll go"

This journey is hard enough without the clinic adding stress and upset. Thankfully I have the best dad in the world, who not only gets me through every single day, but offered to pay to take our last Frosty private.

What a guy

It was a really daunting thought to move private and out of the NHS because once you start spending money on IVF when do you stop?! How far do you go with it?? I had always thought that we wouldn't have to get to that stage, we had two stimulations with plenty of Frosties, but after 5 transfers,4 confirmed miscarriages and a few cancelled due to illness here we are. We are at the stage I thought we never would be.

I continue to watch other people's treatment work first time, unbelievably happy for all these people but also sad for us. We continue to see people conceive naturally (again very happy for them) We continue to live with the fear that this may never work for us, for me! I've gained a new fear this last year, What if he leaves me? And gets someone else pregnant! Now this is ridiculous because my OH loves me and I know that but this journey puts such a strain on you, as a couple we have become stronger through it and he supports me but it's getting serious now and I'm scared. All the time. Scared of all the different outcomes that are out of our control but after 4 years of IVF who wouldn't be scared. Its all just part and parcel of infertility, apparently I'm not classed as "Infertile" I am classed as Sub-fertile. I can't get pregnant without help but that doesn't mean I won't, I just haven't yet.

We chose to go to Knutsford for our private treatment and we couldn't fault them. Our consultant was great from the moment we met him. Straight away he gave me a box of Infolic to start taking as he believes it will help me. If your trying to conceive or you're on treatment look it up because it's got a lot of benefits. We discussed our history and we discussed how to proceed. I had suggested being put on blood thinners as that had worked for a friend of mine. He didn't believe it would make a difference but also it wouldn't do any harm so added it to our treatment plan mainly for my peace of mind. To strike off an unnecessary "what if" So we booked in a specialist courier to pick up our little embryo from Manchester and take a day trip down the motorway to its new home.

The time has come, Day 1 of our last treatment, with our last embryo, what could be my last chance of becoming a mum. It really does feel like this one is my last chance of being a mum. I know there is surrogacy and adoption or another stimulation to consider but if this one doesn't work I have to be tested for NATURAL KILLER CELLS. Which may be the cause of me losing the embryos by 10dp transfer onwards. Basically, my body sees the embryo as a foreign body and kills it. Great for cancer though as my body would fight it instantly if I do have them, silver lining.

I sit waiting for my scan at my shiny new clinic getting checked to make sure my womb, cervix and lining are all ok to start on my next cycle. I got really poorly on my medicated FET so this Consultant has changed it up a bit (thank god) Progynova tablets from Day1, the wonderful butt bullets that ruin your life called Cyclogest. And a blood thinner called Clexane which I start the day of transfer. I am also booking acupuncture for the day of transfer, you have one session before you go in and one when you come out, so hopefully these changes will be the changes we need for our little miracle to stick and stay.

The first week of Progynova went quite well really, probably the best I have ever felt on any of my medications. I even managed to do a 5hr Aerobathon for charity over the weekend. Boobs massive and sore as always so I bought some comfy aka non-sexy bras much to OH's disgust but my boobies delight. But other than that I feel pretty good. Bit emotional on and off but think that's more down to the situation than the meds...or maybe it's a bit of both.

Scan day arrived and the consultant told me my lining was 8.6mm and beautiful. Never had my uterus called that before. Because my lining was so beautiful, we got booked in for our transfer.

Our last embryo!! Lucky number 9?

Chapter 18

Tale as old as time

Our Frostie has survived defrosting. After a very anxious morning of waiting at 9.40am they rang me and I was on pins waiting for them to say it hadn't survived. Well it was just a consent call to make sure we wanted them to go ahead with the thaw...YES PLEASE! So they advised me they would call in an hour to let us know if we are ok to set off. Now if you say you're going to call in an hour, call in an hour. We have a 1.5hour drive and an hour's acupuncture beforehand. 2HOURS40MINUTES later they ring. "Sorry was a bit of a delay" A BIT!! Might only be 1hr40mins over for you but in those 100minutes I'd given up all hope that it had survived. So she got a bit of a sharp tongue but the fact it had survived lifted my mood immediately so she got off lightly to be fair (don't annoy a hormonal mess)

Off we go.....Acupuncture booked for 2/2.15pm and transfer at 3pm

The transfer went really well, I was so relaxed after the acupuncture and because they staff were only dealing with 1 patient at a time you didn't feel like number in a cattle market. The whole experience was just so much calmer and professional which is so reassuring.

10mins later and we were PUPO, our grade 5BA 5day hatching Blastocyst was in place and ready to fight to be our miracle.

2 week wait here we come. It's actually not 2 weeks at this clinic its 10days, 4 whole days less. When they told me that I nearly hugged the nurse. We travelled home and I had few days to relax and help the little one stick before I go back to work.

5DP5DT up 5am, bad sleep and nightmares have started again. I got such bad aches going down my legs. It was like a nerve was trapped or like when your legs are going dead (weird & annoying) I tried sleeping with a pillow between my legs to ease my hip pains and that seemed to work.

So the first 5days after transfer I would wake up with aches in lower abdomen and lower back, pretty sure I was implanting (I'm crazy I know) but I'm pretty convinced I was. Our dog was weird from day 4, She knows!! (I know - I'm crazy) but she knows! Even OH is convinced we're pregnant because of her behaviour. That night she literally just sat staring at me for ages just sat there and followed me everywhere, wouldn't leave my side she even came upstairs following me and she knows she's not allowed upstairs!

Symptoms wise I had on and off nausea all day and night, worse at night. Sore & large boobies as per usual. Felt hungry all the time but would feel full quickly. I ate a share bag of Max Crisps Jalapeno and cheese flavour every day for the 10days, cue the whale look. I had a stitch like feeling in my left side which wouldn't shift. I found it so strange to have all these symptoms because if I was TTC naturally surely, I wouldn't have felt them so early. It must be because we have medications on top of the hormones pregnancy causes therefore heightening everything because my pelvis/hips/stomach/legs ache like crazy which seems odd when the baby (yes I know it's too early to be called a baby) is the size of a seed.

Day 7 PANIC STATIONS PEOPLE.

Can you guess what's happening?? Yep you guessed it again I am spotting, although I am pretty convinced at this point that it is an implantation bleed. Because this is our time so that is what it has to be. But I am starting to cramp. Could be a good sign, could be a bad sign. The standard conflict of symptoms, Pregnancy v Period v Butt Bullets. Well I am just going to have to test early aren't I. What else could I do? How else would I stop myself panicking?

I get up and test, in secret obviously. Two very faint lines. I am pregnant.

But very faintly pregnant. The lines were there but barely. Which meant one of two things. One: I have only just implanted so I am only just pregnant and the lines will be stronger in 2days. Two: I implanted on Day 4 like I suspected and its going horribly wrong already.

OTD is upon us.

BFN (big fat negative) the dream is over. Our last embryo, our last chance, our last bit of hope, gone. There's that pain again, That moment when you can actually feel the pain in your chest when your heart breaks.

What are we supposed to do now?

The only thing we can do. Heal.

On May 4th 2019 something changed in me and I lost all the fight I had in me. I hated myself. I hated my body. I hated what my body was doing to me, to us. Feeling like such a failure. Feeling pointless. Feeling worthless. Nothing or nobody was going to be able to change how I was feeling, the only thing that would help me is time. Tale as old as time as they say.

I am pleased to say over time I healed. It was a hard-long struggle and our relationship was put to the test but we survived at the skin of our teeth. We love each other and that's that, sometimes you feel like love isn't enough and it would be easy to give up, but we made it, in fact I am now "Mrs Dunderdale to be". I am so lucky to have such an amazing group of friends and family in my life. I would never have got through all of this without them. I won't list them all because they know who they are. But thank you to you all.

So what's next I hear you say??

I guess we will find out in book number 2 (wink*wink)

I will continue this fight…..until that last petal falls

Cover designed by Denise Taylor

Cover Illustrated

By

Sophie Holman

Flourish Illustrations

Email

untilthelastpetalfalls@yahoo.com

Website/Blog

www.untilthelastpetalsfalls.wordpress.com

Please follow me on Instagram

@ivf_untilthelastpetalfalls

COMING SOON

"A Dream is a wish your heart makes"

Until the last petal falls Part 2

Printed in Germany
by Amazon Distribution
GmbH, Leipzig